Original title:
Life in the Terrarium

Copyright © 2025 Creative Arts Management OÜ
All rights reserved.

Author: Adeline Fairfax
ISBN HARDBACK: 978-1-80581-895-3
ISBN PAPERBACK: 978-1-80581-422-1
ISBN EBOOK: 978-1-80581-895-3

Sheltered Spheres of Existence

In a glassy dome, the critters scheme,
They plan their plot while I just dream.
The snail's a philosopher, slow yet wise,
While the ants hold meetings under bright skies.

With moss for couches and pebbles for chairs,
They gossip in whispers, with no worldly cares.
An earthworm muses on matters profound,
In their little bubble, joy's always found.

Verdant Echoes in a Small World

A frog croaks jokes, quite ribbeting fun,
By the pebble pond, they bask in the sun.
A busy bee buzzes, "What's the latest scoop?"
While the lizard does yoga in a leafy loop.

Mossy landscapes hide tales from a leaf,
Silly tiny dramas, all comic relief.
In this tiny cosmos, they dance and they play,
My little green pals, they brighten my day.

The Oasis Within the Crystal

Within clear walls, a jungle thrives,
Cockroaches dance, oh how they jive!
A tiny sun shines on the wispy grass,
While the eager beetles have a race to pass.

A ladybug laughs, 'What's under your shell?'
The spiders weave webs, all is swell.
In this oasis, they rule the domain,
With jokes and giggles, they've nothing to gain.

Bound by Glass, Free in Spirit

Within a box, these critters tweet,
A parakeet philosopher, busy and sweet.
A hermit crab moves, changing its home,
While the fish swims circles, as if to roam.

The world outside seems big and bleak,
But here there's laughter, with every squeak.
They may be trapped in a world so small,
Yet in their own way, they're having a ball.

The Glassy Veil of Habitat

In a glass box, plants dance about,
Critters scurry, full of doubt.
A mossy kingdom, tiny and bright,
Sunlit battles, a comical sight.

Frogs leap high with swaggering flair,
While ants march on without a care.
A lizard grins, basking with glee,
Who knew a jar could hold such a spree?

Fragile Ecosystems

Tiny worlds, all packed in tight,
Squabbles over food, what a sight!
The snail's slow race, a memorable scene,
With a cocky beetle, bold and mean.

A plant whispers gossip of the bugs,
While earthworms give sneaky, sly shrugs.
Rooftops of soil, a kingdom of fun,
Where promises of chaos are never done.

Enduring Tales

What tales these glassy walls could tell,
Of crazy critters who wish me well.
A spider spins tales of woe and delight,
While the fish makes faces, putting up a fight.

Each droplet of water, a laugh or a tear,
As creatures embark on journeys unclear.
A snail with a hat, so proud and so bold,
In a world that feels slightly controlled.

Encased Growths and Wandering Thoughts

A mossy carpet, it catches the eye,
While the caterpillar thinks it can fly.
Greens intertwine with creativity flair,
While every critter hides from despair.

The snappy plants plot little tricks,
As frogs and beetles engage in quick flicks.
In this little realm, laughter runs free,
Oh, the antics of these friends, such glee!

Whispers of Water and Soil

Bubbles giggle, beneath the glass dome,
As roots wriggle, feeling at home.
Water droplets whisper secrets of cheer,
While the whole scene bursts with giggles and sneers.

The tiny inhabitants play hide and seek,
In this quirky theatre, unique and chic.
Earthworms engaged in deep discussion,
Where nonsense reigns—oh, what a production!

Living Stillness

In a glass box where all is bright,
Mini monsters roam day and night.
A snail on a mission, taking its time,
While tiny ants form a parade line.

Frogs discuss what's hip in the shade,
While a lizard's dance is grandly displayed.
A plant throws shade, with a leafy grin,
As cockroaches ponder where to begin.

Enchanted Within the Walls

Beneath the glass, the critters play,
In a surreal dance beneath the ray.
A beetle's stuck in a leaf so grand,
While mice debate who's in command.

Moss wigs out as it gets too warm,
And ferns giggle in a gentle swarm.
A spider weaves tales of daring feats,
As crickets accompany with rhythmic beats.

Nature's Microcosm

A kingdom ruled by insects small,
Where grasshoppers boldly stand tall.
The cucumber beetles have a ball,
While ants gossip, the queens rise and fall.

A chatty worm claims it's the king,
While flies dance, making quite the swing.
The soil grins, knowing it's the host,
While everyone cheers for the fungus toast.

Serenity in the Sealed Space

In this tiny world, no one is late,
As geraniums argue the best of fate.
A chubby toad takes a midday snooze,
While ladybugs share their colorful views.

Bubbles rise from the gassy dirt,
As things wiggle and give a flirt.
The roaches play peek-a-boo all day,
In this glass palace where we laugh and stay.

Aromas of a Controlled Climate

In glassy halls where plants pretend,
They whisper secrets, roots to send.
A sprout winks at the sunlit sky,
While snails zoom by on a leafy high.

The air is thick with earthy cheer,
While lizards lounge with a froggy leer.
Moss throws parties, all plush and green,
And bugs do salsa, a wild scene!

A tiny world with rules divine,
Where random sprouts sip on sunshine.
Petunia giggles, the violets grin,
As they throw shade at the thick skinned kin.

Sometimes it rains—oh what a hoot!
The ferns just dance in their bootless roots.
While creatures peek from their cozy beds,
And ponder life's truths with wiggly heads.

Cradled Nature within Boundaries

In a glass box where shadows play,
Critters scurry in their leafy ballet.
The peas plead for sunlight's warm kiss,
While carrots dig in, a rooty bliss.

A snail slides by with a slow-motion flair,
Gossiping mushrooms with a scandalous stare.
The humidity wraps all in a hug,
As cyclamen giggles—oh what a rug!

Tiny hearts beat beneath the glow,
As lilies knit tales of joy and woe.
Each leaf a chapter, each petal a joke,
In whispered giggles, the plants all invoke.

A fish peeks through at the curious scene,
While ants hold court like they're all routines.
Oh, this glass world is a rollicking feast,
Where the smallest of creatures dance—at least!

Petals in a Polished Prison

Behind the glass, flowers get high,
With bees as their bouncers, flying by.
Each petal shines, a vibrant cheer,
As spiders spin tales—oh dear, oh dear!

The wise old fern advises all,
Don't bend too low or you might fall.
The tranquility here, quite absurd,
As the ferns sing songs—just listen to the word!

A plant once dreamed of a big escape,
But realized its roots made things take shape.
So it relaxes, drinks raindrops fine,
While blooms make jokes over dinner wine.

And every day, a new game unfolds,
With mud and laughter, laughter that molds.
The beetles groove in their party attire,
In this polished chamber, never to tire!

Eden Encased in Transparency

In a crystal grotto where giggles swell,
The mushroom munchkins cast their spell.
Frogs on stilts leap over logs,
As daisies giggle at passing dogs.

The ukelele moss strikes a tune,
While a ladybug dances, round like a moon.
The air is thick with jokes untold,
As roots entangle in their green gold.

The grasshoppers chirp their own delight,
In this tiny world, there's no fight.
Each bloom a custodian of light and cheer,
Delivering laughs that all can hear.

A curtain of glass keeps the chaos at bay,
While crickets converse, simply enjoying the day.
So here they frolic, intertwining fate,
In this little wonderland, never too late!

Enclosure of Organic Tales

In a glass box, critters prance,
Fern and moss engage in dance.
Cactus waving, pine cones sway,
Who knew plants could act this way?

Tiny snails with great delight,
Race on leaves, a comical sight.
A squirrel peeks from leafy shade,
Planning mischief? Never displayed!

Jars are homes for quirky bugs,
Who share their space with little mugs.
Every drop of water counts,
Counting laughs as humor mounts!

Bumblebees do the cha-cha-cha,
Under twinkling stars, hurrah!
With every bloom, a tale unfolds,
In a home made of glass, so bold!

Elysium in a Glass Chamber

A beetle reads the morning news,
While ants on tiny bikes amuse.
Poked by twigs, a snail plays shy,
"Leave me be, I'm not that spry!"

Sunlight streams, the lizards bask,
While plushy frogs engage in tasks.
In this space, the dance is grand,
Wiggly worms lead a funky band.

Daisies gossip, roots entwine,
"Did you hear? The bugs are fine!"
Petal parties, pop the cheer,
In their world, no room for fear!

Amidst the growth, a snail will sigh,
"Why is the green always so spry?"
With laughter among boughs and leaves,
It's a world that never grieves!

The Tranquility of Captive Growths

In a tank where greens outshine,
Tiny gnomes sip sweet sunshine.
A keystone cop of garden glee,
Chasing shadows, oh so free!

Mighty ferns wave to and fro,
While mossy pillows steal the show.
In little pots, a ruckus brews,
With happy roots in weekend shoes.

Laughter bubbles through the glass,
With every critter taking sass.
A squirrel cracks jokes at full speed,
As peas rush by, oh what a creed!

Charming weeds have a fun spree,
"Why do we live here? Who's the bee?"
In the joy of growth, no haste,
Each moment, a delightful taste!

Growing Beneath the Veil

In glassy homes where squirrels can't roam,
The plants tell secrets, never alone.
Ferns wear their fronds like party hats,
While tiny bugs throw wild, tiny chats.

Spiders weave stories, intricate and tight,
While moss keeps the whispers, all through the night.
A lizard struts, a fashionable gent,
Claiming each leaf for his royal content.

The sun peeks in with a playful grin,
While water droplets work to begin.
Every root wiggles in carpet of joy,
An underground ruckus, like kids with a toy.

So laugh with the greens, join in their play,
In the little world, where the odd laugh and sway.
For who would have thought, in a world so small,
Such hilarious beings could thrive for us all?

Nature's Dance in Miniature

In a jar of glass where no one can hide,
The creatures get busy, with nowhere to bide.
A snail slides through like he's on a slick race,
While ants practice tango, all over the place.

The ladybugs boast of their spotted arrays,
While worms do a jig in the damp, shadowy bays.
With each little rumble, a creature jumps high,
To catch the attention of a curious fly.

Then here comes a beetle, in heels of pure gold,
Declaring his entrance—'Behold! I am bold!'
The plants sway in rhythm, the soil holds its breath,
As nature puts on quite the show, not to rest.

So peek in your glass, let laughter arise,
At the shenanigans played before your eyes.
The showcase of nature, so small yet so grand,
Will fill up your heart with a joke, so unplanned!

The Enclosed Eden

Inside this dome where the green things grow,
Life zooms about, putting on quite a show.
The spider, with flair, spins webs made of dreams,
While crickets recite poetry softly, it seems.

Each bead of dew shines like diamonds anew,
As plants giggle gently, sharing their view.
A frog in a pot considers a leap,
While watching the ants' marathon, never to sleep.

Caterpillars plan their big butterfly flight,
As water gives kisses to honor the night.
The pebbles have meetings, oh what do they share?
The drama of roots and a dance to declare!

So come for a visit, but mind your own tune,
For the fun never ends in this glassy cocoon.
With laughter and mischief, you can't help but see,
This Eden of goofiness thrives joyfully!

Fragments of Green Enchantment

Tiny worlds hidden under the glass dome,
Where creatures concoct a plan for their home.
A dancing plant waved, as if it could talk,
It whispered sweet secrets, and laughed as it walked.

The rocks tell a tale of the years they've survived,
While a beetle debates how to thrive and contrive.
A squirrel watches close from the outside, with glee,
As he plots to outsmart this vibrant mini sea.

With catchy tunes from the bumblebee band,
And petals that sway with a rhythm so grand,
Each inch has a story, a chuckle, a smile,
The magic of green goes on all the while.

So take a short trip where the funny things play,
In the cracks and the crevices, joy leaps and sways.
A cheer from the earth as the sunlight does beam,
In this world of enchantment, you're living the dream!

Breath of the Contained Forest

In a glass box, green things thrive,
A tiny world where plants connive.
Snails in tuxedos slide with grace,
While ants plot mischief in their space.

Frogs play leapfrog, oh what a show,
With mossy carpets, they steal the glow.
A squirrel's kick, a leaf does flip,
In this miniature, nature's quip.

Worms party hard beneath the ground,
While roots converse in whispers found.
The crickets' song, a quirky tune,
Underneath a bright, plastic moon.

So let's arrange a soirée here,
Invite these critters, lend your ear.
For in this glassy paradise,
Each day's a laugh, without disguise.

Serenity in a Soil-bound Space

In the small patch where shadows play,
Sunbeams dance at the end of the day.
The tiny trees are taking bets,
On which of them will grow the best.

A beetle dons a silly hat,
While worms do a conga, imagine that!
In the soil, mischief flows like wine,
With roots intertwining, looking divine.

Now and then, a dragonfly swoops,
In a blur, it dodges the gathering troops.
Ladybugs share giggles and glee,
As they plot the best view from the pea.

In this quaint plot, no room for gloom,
As laughter fills every little bloom.
Let's cherish the chaos and silly clout,
In our soft, soil-bound, playful bout.

Microcosmic Whispers of Spring

Springtime whispers in the small,
With tiny buds that start to sprawl.
A frog tells jokes with croaky glee,
While flowers tiptoe, oh so free.

Mice play hide-and-seek by the stone,
Forging friendships, never alone.
Tiny paws and wings collide,
In the thicket where dreams reside.

Bees decorously strut their stuff,
Buzzing around, never too rough.
A patch of grass holds an open mic,
Where every sound deserves a hike.

This liveliness in such a small place,
Makes every heart race in this space.
So gather 'round, both big and small,
In this world, we're having a ball!

Creatures of the Glassy Realm

In a chamber where critters collide,
Dancing shadows playfully hide.
A snail's slow poke is a fancy race,
While spiders spin threads with style and grace.

Tiny turtles, their heads like a dome,
Climbing rocks, they call it home.
In the corners, the shrew takes bets,
On who'll trip over the cobweb nets.

Lizards bask under warm sun rays,
With silly grins, enjoying the craze.
The air smells sweet with leafy snacks,
As chubby pill bugs keep up with tracks.

So here's to the creatures, both wild and free,
In this glassy kingdom, you'll find glee.
Let's raise a toast with tiny cheers,
For laughter blooms through the glassy years.

Bridging Nature and Containment

Inside a glass box, plants take a leap,
Sharing their secrets while we snooze and sleep.
A tiny jungle where chaos is nice,
And moss makes a sofa—now that's living spice!

Pet snail named Gary runs track on the floor,
While orchids gossip, their petals explore.
With tiny insects playing peek-a-boo,
In this glassy abode, we bid you adieu!

The Eternal Dance of the Enclosed

Beneath the glass dome, a party in green,
Plants shimmy and shake—what a vibrant scene!
The ferns throw a rave, while the cacti just sigh,
And the mushrooms giggle, oh my, oh my!

The lizard, a DJ, scratches with glee,
To the sound of a breeze that nobody hears but me.
With pots as their partners, they twirl and they glide,
In a world so contained, happiness can't hide.

A Tranquil Oasis Behind Glass

A glassy retreat, where quietness reigns,
Where flora and fauna relax without chains.
The goldfish is king, with a crown made of foam,
While the plants plot a coup, claiming this home!

The turtle lazily spins in his bowl,
While marbles and pebbles play hide and roll.
A drama unfolds as the sunlight reveals,
The gossip of greens about how this feels!

Surrounded by Verdant Whispers

Whispers of greenery in dollhouse design,
Where snails plot world travel, but can't find the time.
The succulents puzzle over their prickly attire,
While moss, in its wisdom, inspires desire!

The frogs hold a meeting, discussing the past,
The shadows grow tall; the tiniest cast.
In this playful haven, humor in each nook,
A terrarium tale in a storybook!

Molecular Gardens of Delight

In jars of glass, they wiggle and sway,
A tiny dance, they amuse all day.
With snacks of moss and sips of dew,
They throw a party for just a few.

A critter here, a critter there,
With fuzzy friends on a maiden fair.
They gossip about the world outside,
While we just laugh, they giggle and hide.

A kingdom small, a vibrant scene,
Where nothing's ever truly mean.
They orchestrate a tiny plot,
Oh, what a show! We love their lot!

When lights go out, they snicker and tease,
In their living room, they do just as they please.
With laughter booming within the glass,
The garden's humor is sure to last!

The Symphony of Miniature Ecosystems

In tiny worlds, the creatures bop,
Each leaf a stage, they never stop.
A thimble-sized frog plays a sweet tune,
While ants do the cha-cha by the moon.

The moss takes a bow, the ferns applaud,
Dancing under the beam of a flashlight's nod.
With beetles drumming on the soil so fine,
It's a concert that's truly divine!

The ladybugs strut, the spiders swing,
A minuscule dance in a leafy ring.
With laughter echoed in every nook,
Who knew nature could be such a kook?

As the curtain falls on their leafy plight,
They all retire for a restful night.
In their human-sized world, we see their glee,
Oh, the joy in their symphony carefree!

Shadows of the Enclosed Wilderness

In shadowy corners, secrets abound,
A cabal of critters silently found.
Geckos in suits and snakes in ties,
Exchanging their whispers and knowing sighs.

The shadows twirl, a waltz so sly,
While the crickets in whispers comply.
With gentle nudges, a critter slips,
To take part in the midnight quips.

Tiny owls hoot in playful tones,
While crabs play chess on marvelous stones.
With humor dripping like morning dew,
The shadows laugh when the morn breaks through!

When sunlight bursts through the glassy dome,
These jesters flee to make their home.
Yet in the quiet, their chuckles remain,
In the realm where shadows stake their claim!

Verdant Hopes in a Diminutive Space

In a pint-sized world, dreams take root,
Where tiny sprouts wear their leafy suit.
With aspirations as wide as a sea,
These green little hopes giggle with glee.

The beetles debate who's the fastest sprinter,
While worms critique the latest winter.
With hopes so high in a container small,
They search for the sun to embrace them all.

Amidst the greens, the fun never ends,
As frogs claim thrones, and vines condescend.
There's humor in every droplet glint,
As tiny dreams blossom—so bold, so mint!

As dusk settles in, they hold a ball,
Swinging the night in their colorful hall.
In this diminutive space, joy flows free,
A verdant utopia—what a sight to see!

Lush Chronicles of Enclosure

When mossy parties get too loud,
The shy old snail just hides, quite proud.
The crickets joke about the glow,
While beetles dance in quite a show.

A cactus wears a tiny hat,
With spiky friends, they chit and chat.
The little lizard, quick and spry,
Claims he can leap, but oh, he's shy.

A tortoise trots with all his grace,
While wishing he could pick up pace.
The plants all laugh and sway in cheer,
As if to say, "We have no fear!"

With every wiggle, hop, and crawl,
This leafy world holds fun for all.
The jolly critters make their mark,
In this bright box, where laughter sparks.

Reflections of a Leafy Sanctuary

In corners where the shadows play,
A fern declares it's party day.
The raccoons with their masks so bright,
Steal snacks, it's quite a funny sight.

Old Mr. Toad sings out of tune,
While bugs jump up to join the swoon.
The pebbles roll and giggle on,
As if to say, "Come join the fun!"

A butterfly attempts to twirl,
But lands too hard, it sends her whirl.
With giggles shared among the leaves,
This sanctuary never grieves.

So grab a twig, and come on down,
To join the laughter all around.
In this green space, joy's unfurled,
A quirky, charming little world.

Hidden Realms of Biodiversity

The ants play cards beneath a vine,
While snails decide their next design.
A ladybug lands with a wink,
And shouts, "I'm here! Come grab a drink!"

The lizards share a stand-up show,
With punchlines that just might steal the show.
A squirrel's pranks with acorns fly,
As giggles fill the open sky.

The roots below do twist and twirl,
Creating scenes in this small world.
A flower whispers, "What's the scoop?"
While ferns just sway and form a loop.

The mossy couch invites a rest,
As critters gather, feeling blessed.
In hidden nooks, there's much to find,
A silly place for all so kind.

The Stillness of a Closed Canopy

In the quiet hush of leafy heights,
A squirrel ponders her late-night bites.
A breeze shakes melodious leaves,
As the cardinals share their thieves.

The shadows dance with teasing flair,
As quiet schemes float through the air.
The beetles hum a secret tune,
With witty lines to make you swoon.

A feathered friend can't find the door,
While chuckling flowers beg for more.
In stillness, laughter brews and grows,
As every petal knows what shows.

The world above may seem serene,
But underneath, it's a jolly scene.
With every crack and creak and sigh,
This canopy holds laughter nigh.

Tread Softly in this Enclosed Wilderness

In a glass box where critters roam,
A squirrel steals snacks, it's no longer alone.
A frog in a hat croaks jokes with flair,
As turtles debate who sits in a chair.

The moss is a carpet, fresh from a sale,
While snails race to win a speedboat's tail.
Inside this bubble, where everyone thrives,
Even the ants keep track of their jives.

Blooming Whimsies Under a Dome

Petals giggle as they wiggle about,
A flower's stuck inside, let it out!
Bees wear shades; they're too cool for school,
While ladybugs plot to rule the whole pool.

Tiny trees whisper to moss-covered stones,
"You're so lazy, just chilling like drones!"
A tumble of leaves recounts an old tale,
While the wind simply giggles, giving them a sail.

Colorful Stillness in Bio-Dome Landscapes

The rocks throw a party, lit up like stars,
While crickets pull pranks and race tiny cars.
A caterpillar thinks it's a butterfly gem,
As plants roll their eyes at the chaos they stem.

Silly grasshoppers form a dance troupe,
While a snail steals the show with its slow, groovy loop.
In this vibrant world, all laugh and play,
Where bubbles of joy pop in a charming array.

Resilience in a Crystal Sphere

In a globe of glass where dreams swirl and spin,
A fish flips and flops, hoping to win.
With a grin on its face, it swims in loops,
While cacti keep track of all the good scoops.

A hedgehog in shades gives life all it's got,
Chasing down laughter in a world that's so hot.
Mushrooms hold meetings under the bright sun,
While the lizards debate who ought to have fun.

The Enchantment of the Enclosed

In a glassy bubble, critters prance,
A snail in a party hat begins to dance.
Frogs croak jokes with a melodic quirk,
While ants debate who will do the work.

Lush green ferns wave like a cavalcade,
As beetles throw shade in their funky parade.
Temperature's rising, the humidity's wild,
A cactus just gave birth to a spiky child.

Melodies of Moisture and Light

Sunlight kisses leaves like a friendly tease,
Moss sings softly, 'Hey, do you smell the breeze?'
Water droplets dance on the glassy floor,
Every sunny moment is never a bore.

The temperature rises, a chorus of cheers,
As crickets play tunes ringing in your ears.
If you peek inside, you might just find,
A lizard doing yoga, quite unconfined.

Surviving in a Transparent Sphere

In a clear dome, the air is thick,
A dragonfly's here, oh what a trick!
He plays hide and seek under glossy leaves,
While a timid worm writes poetry that weaves.

The light's always right for a fun little chat,
With spiders who spin tales, then pounce like a cat.
A ladybug's giggle echoes through the air,
'Who knew being critters could be so rare?'

Secrets of the Terracotta Refuge

In pots of clay where secrets crawl,
The tales of plants hold a festival ball.
A row of daisies gossip and laugh,
While terrain folks plot, crafting their craft.

The beans are dreaming of heights so grand,
While fungus interrupts with an uninvited hand.
'Hey you, green thumb! Come watch us grow,'
Said the cactus, blushing, as sunlight stole the show.

Echoes of Nature's Embrace

A tiny snail with quite a tale,
Racing roots, oh what a fail!
Said the frog with a croak so bold,
"I'll see you later, I'm off to mold!"

Tiny ants in disciplined lines,
Carrying crumbs, oh what designs!
A wardrobe mishap with the dirt,
Dancing worms in their fancy shirt.

A cacti outburst, saying "Yikes!"
Sipping water in tiny spikes.
Moss giggles under the moonlight's beam,
"We're all part of someone's quirky dream!"

In this glass bubble they all convene,
Staging drama, a rare scene.
Nature's jesters play without a cause,
Amidst the laughter of leaves and paws.

The Small Universe Flourishing

In a jar it's a world so small,
A lizard's dance, who knew he'd fall?
Potted plants plan their great escape,
Plotting paths like a leafy landscape.

Mighty mushrooms with their hats in tow,
Hoping to start a show for the crow.
A spider spins tales so absurd,
"This is the best, haven't you heard?"

A rock that dreams to be more than stone,
Mocking the plants, "You're never alone!"
While crickets converse about life's grand scheme,
As fireflies twinkle, just living the dream.

In this little cosmos, who'd make a fuss?
All creatures living in blissful plus.
Chasing their shadows, a curious bunch,
Every day's a party, just wait for the lunch.

Terracotta Dreams in a Jar

In terracotta pots they share a joke,
While a weary cactus starts to poke.
Terms of endearment, a sweet serenade,
Listen closely; the plants have it made!

Tomato vines reach for the sky,
A radish whispers, "Don't be shy!"
Silly beetles cast shadows galore,
Pretending they're knights, ready to soar.

Neighbors argue who gets the sun,
"I swear it's hotter! I'm just having fun!"
A tiny snail with dreams of a race,
Rolling on wheels, what a funny place!

Their terracotta home, a goofy dream,
Life tumbles on, an endless theme.
Each petal giggles, each leaf plays a role,
In this quirky world, there's joy in the whole.

Enchanted Growth Behind Windows

Behind the glass, a buzzing spree,
Toadstools gossip, "Look at me!"
Sunlight tickles their leafy toes,
Daisy throws a party, everyone knows.

Potting soil sings a funky beat,
A squirrel peeks in, thinking it's neat.
In the sun, the roses yawn and sway,
"Let's invite the sunbirds to our play!"

A coconut shell rolls by in a glint,
Chasing shadows, old as a print.
The butterfly's laugh, a sweet little tune,
Dancing in sync with the bright afternoon.

Beneath the rain, they chuckle in glee,
Expecting a joke from the old bumblebee.
In this patch, where dreams intertwine,
A whimsical world, just sipping on sunshine.

Sanctuary of the Silent

In a glass box, critters convene,
Tiny lizards, all so keen.
They plot and scheme, but who will hear?
The whirring sound of a distant gear.

Moss becomes the carpet, soft and neat,
While crickets dance with tap-tap feet.
The snail's slow race is a glorious sight,
He wins, of course, by taking all night.

A leaf falls down like a stealthy ninja,
The worm thinks, 'Hey! I'm a real defender!'
But when it lands, oh what a fuss,
They lose their groove, it's a big plus!

Dew drops glitter, like tiny stars,
While ants debate the best of bars.
Each day's a contest soaked in glee,
In this sanctuary, wild and free!

Oasis of the Overlooked

Tiny cacti in a plushy row,
Sipping sunshine, putting on a show.
Their spines are sharp, but hearts are light,
A prickly club, a bit of fright.

A beetle stumbles on a pebble stash,
And good old Mr. Frog, he starts to laugh.
With bulging eyes and a goofy grin,
The dance-off starts—let's begin!

Bright blooms gossip with the breeze,
"Did you hear about the ants? Oh please!"
They wiggle and giggle, sharing the scoop,
As the tiniest critters form a happy troop.

In the shadows, sly and wise,
A turtle watches the grand surprise.
He shouts, "Rotate! You gotta see,
An oasis here, just for me!

Whispers of the Glass Garden

In a glass world filled with glee,
Funky plants grow wild and free.
Mossy carpets, a plush delight,
Even worms have their spotlights!

A festival for ants takes flight,
In search of crumbs—it's a tasty night.
Stretched-out leaves, the perfect stage,
They shake their legs and dance with rage!

Grasshoppers laugh with a chirpy tune,
Under the glow of a silvery moon.
They debate if they hop or just stand,
With ridiculous stunts, they all take a hand.

In this glass garden, quirks collide,
Where awkward creatures simply abide.
With smiles broad, they share their song,
Whispers in green, where all belong!

Secrets Under the Dome

Beneath the dome, chaos unfolds,
Silly secrets that nature holds.
The beetles boast, "I'm king of cool!"
While the spider crafts a cozy spool.

A roach makes rounds, a random guest,
"Who's hosting tonight? I'm feeling blessed!"
The ferns all wave, they're part of the crew,
With the moss providing a lovely view.

Each corner has a tale to share,
Of tiny pranks and leafy dare.
A snail races to claim the throne,
But ends up getting lost—alone!

Frogs croak jokes that never land,
While grass blades form the marching band.
Secrets bloom in this quirky hold,
Under the dome, strange tales unfold.

Glass Gardens Unveiled

In a jar where sunlight beams,
Tiny wonders plot their schemes.
Frogs in suits play cards all day,
While snails slide by, just want to play.

A cactus wears a tiny hat,
And wonders where the breezes at.
Bubbles dance, a fish's cheer,
In glassy worlds, there's naught to fear.

A curious beetle shimmies near,
As crickets strum without a care.
Lizards lounge on comfy rocks,
While ants do math with crazy clocks.

Dancers whirl in leafy rooms,
As nature's laughter brightly blooms.
In this realm of glass and green,
All is fun, and yet serene.

Beings in a Crystal Chamber

Inside this orb, the fun unfolds,
With tales of tiny creatures bold.
A mouse in slippers, quite a sight,
While geckos toast with juice at night.

The goldfish jokes with wise old snails,
As ants retell their daring tales.
A gnome tries fixing broken lights,
But ends up tangled in plant kites.

Frogs jump high with leaps of cheer,
While bees debate the best soft beer.
In crystal air, they share their dreams,
In a world that glitters, it always seems.

Mice write songs on tiny leaves,
Their melodies, a charm, it weaves.
In chambers bright with laughter's glow,
Their spirits dance, a funny show.

Whispers Among the Moss

There's gossip here beneath the rocks,
Where slugs hold court, and time mock clocks.
Mossy whispers float like dreams,
As critters plot their crafty schemes.

A worm claims fame in silky threads,
While spiders boast of tangled beds.
Grasshoppers leap with comic flair,
As toads chime in without a care.

The vibrant greens, a troupe on stage,
Sharing laughs that never age.
Beneath the leaves, the jokes collide,
In nature's funny, humble tide.

With mushrooms spouting witty puns,
Life is a show—no need for runs.
In shadows deep, the mirth is tossed,
Among the moss, no joy is lost.

Breath of the Enclosed

In this bubble of humid cheer,
A parakeet sings, 'Come have a beer!'
A turtle dressed in vibrant stripes,
Dreams of surfing and all the gripes.

Mice throw parties with cheese galore,
While crickets dance on plants they adore.
A lizard in shades invites the crew,
Saying, "Sunbathing's better with a view!"

Beneath the glass, the antics thrive,
With plants that giggle and critters jive.
Every squeak and chirp, a thrilling game,
In this sealed world, all is the same.

A wink of light, a bit of green,
In laughter's grasp, we find the scene.
So take a breath, join in the fun,
In this cozy bubble, we all are one.

Nature's Cradle

In a jar where plants can thrive,
A tiny world tries to come alive.
With mossy beds and pebbled streams,
They plot their cute and quirky schemes.

The residents dance, a leafy parade,
While gnomes stand guard, never afraid.
A spider spins silk with great flair,
A lizard pretends he doesn't care.

Herbivore snails munch on greens,
While ants conduct secret routines.
Each day a new drama unfolds,
In this glass dome, a story retold.

Worms whisper secrets deep in roots,
As frogs wear their fanciest boots.
A frog that croaks a tiny song,
In this cradle, how can it be wrong?

Symphony of Glass and Green

Within the walls of shining glass,
The tenants frolic, time does pass.
Leaves flit here with giggles clear,
As nature plays a tune to cheer.

A chorus of bubbles rises so bright,
In this tiny world, what a sight!
The sunbeam's touch a warm embrace,
Each critter here finds its own space.

A fern does a little jig and sway,
While the ladybug leads the ballet.
Cacti hum a prickly song,
As crickets chirp along all day long.

Each morning brings a brand new plot,
A game of tag seems like a lot.
What fun it is, this glassy scene,
In our wild world of light and green!

A World Beneath the Dome

Beneath the dome, the party's grand,
Creatures scurry, plants all stand.
Tiny flowers throw confetti high,
As buzzing bees start to fly by.

A turtle rolls like he's on a spree,
While lizards lounge with raucous glee.
The ants parade in single file,
Creating chaos with every mile.

A snail proposes toast with slime,
With mushrooms dancing, keeping time.
The moss giggles with every bump,
As roots keep rhythm, thud and thump.

This world of whimsy grows so bold,
As silly tales of green unfold.
Under glass, oh what a show,
Where every creature steals the glow!

Fragile Ecosystems

A dance of leaves, a nightly rave,
In tiny bowls that sunlight gave.
Gnat friends buzz on a sugar spree,
While earthworms chant in harmony.

The beetle wears a cap made of dew,
With grinning snails, just passing through.
A broken stick becomes a sword,
The battles fought are oh-so-lord!.

Fronds are flapping with great delight,
In this wild realm, party's in sight.
With whispers shared amongst the crowd,
Their laughter echoes, oh so loud!

Yet, fragile threads connect them here,
Each tiny role so very dear.
In these ecosystems made to laugh,
Nature's jesters have the last half!

Habitat of Hope: Suspended Animation

In a glass box, a snail takes a ride,
Twirling past plants, with nowhere to hide.
Twitching its antennae, it looks quite spry,
While the lazy goldfish just swims on by.

Sunlight sneaks in, the moss gives a cheer,
A tiny ant yells, 'Hey, I'm the engineer!'
With tiny tools, it starts to build,
A bridge of crumbs, oh how it's thrilled!

Each day is a show, the lizard's the star,
Leaping for crickets, it's bizarre by far.
The plants just giggle, their leaves all shake,
As they pull pranks on the poor earthworm's wake.

A world in glass, where dreams never die,
Though everyone's just a little too shy.
In this tiny realm, where silliness rules,
Who knew a terrarium could house such fools!

Drifting Dreams in a Green Sanctuary

In a pot sits a frog, quite uneasy,
Croaking jokes that don't seem so breezy.
The mosses all murmur, 'What's that tone?'
'Not funny,' they quip, 'Stay off the phone!'

A chubby hamster spins like a gem,
While the turtle watches, 'You'll never win!'
Yet round and round, they make quite the pair,
Chasing their tails in a rollicking air.

The sunlight bounces off leafy friends,
As the weevil boogies, the laughter transcends.
With fungi and ferns joining the beat,
It's a mini rave; how could it be beat?

But the caterpillar sulks on a leaf,
Wishing for wings, crying, 'This is brief!'
Yet through the laughter, a small spark ignites,
It's all in good fun, on these leafy nights!

The Spheres of Stagnant Time

Bubble-breathing fish do pirouettes,
While the plants gossip and make their bets.
The rocks are on strike, feeling quite grey,
Complaining aloud, 'We need a holiday!'

A hermit crab says, 'I'm new in town!'
'Where's the fun?' asks a snail looking down.
'Let's form a club, with snacks on the side,
And if guests arrive, it's potluck inside!'

Dark clouds pass by, a gecko peeks out,
'Ever heard the one about the spry sprout?'
On a frosty morning, the humor defrosts,
Even a cactus can throw out some jests!

With laughter confined to this dinky glass space,
They plot to escape—oh, what a chase!
Who knew this bickering would end up so fun?
It's a show just for them—hilarity won!

Lushness Within Translucent Walls

In a crisp little world, sunlight does peek,
An iguana sighs, 'I must rethink my technique.'
'Is this all there is? Just salad and light?'
'Can't a scaly dude have a dance party night?'

In a jungle of glass, all creatures conspire,
The ladybugs whisper, 'We'll start a choir!'
A chorus of chirps, oh, it could be grand,
Yet a sleepy tortoise just can't understand.

Plants stretch their arms, rooting for fame,
'These walls won't bind us; we'll rise to acclaim!'
The soil rolls its eyes, 'You're out of your minds,'
And chuckles emerge from the leafy vines.

So inside this sphere, where silliness thrives,
Creatures hold rallies to keep hope alive.
With jests and a giggle, they flourish with glee,
In this patch of green, we are all so free!

Journeys of the Miniature Beings

Tiny travelers roam the glass,
With itty-bitty backpacks made of grass.
They march on pathways of old, dry earth,
In search of treasures, giggles, and mirth.

Each leaf's a mountain, a skyscraper high,
They launch from moss like astronauts fly.
A frog in a teacup? Oh, what a sight!
With a croak like a trumpet, he joins their flight.

Lush Realms Behind the Pane

Beyond the glass, the ferns all wave,
As the gnome in the corner starts to misbehave.
He tumbles and rolls through the jumbled trails,
Chasing after ants with goofy details.

A snail in a race? What a funny thing!
With measures and mocks, he's a slower king.
The beetles cheer on with tiny fans,
As they flip their lids over his slow-paced plans.

Stories of Soil and Sprout

In the underbrush, secrets are stout,
With whispers of veggies daring to sprout.
A carrot tiptoes, a radish runs,
While broccoli flexes, having too much fun!

A worm holds a mic in a tiny cave,
Singing songs of the great sod they crave.
With funky moves under dirt's bright roof,
They throw a party that's quite goof-proof.

The Hidden Wilds Within

Behind the curtains, a jungle they find,
Where every small critter is perfectly blind.
A lizard does yoga; he's quite the star,
While the ants argue why they don't drive cars.

Moss has its gossip, oh what a scene!
As laughter erupts from both bark and green.
With acorn hats and dandelion shoes,
They plan their adventures, they can't lose!

A Haven Within Acerbic Lines

In a glass house, tiny ants parade,
Waging war on crumbs, a savory crusade.
A guppy in the corner, judging my style,
With a bubble or two, it cracks a big smile.

The cacti gossip, poking fun at me,
'Stop watering us; we prefer to be free!'
A snail's slow dance is a comical sight,
As I sip my tea in the soft morning light.

The hamster wheezes, races 'round the wheel,
While the goldfish plots a grand escape with zeal.
All within glass walls, it's a circus of cheer,
Each day's a new act, with silliness near.

So here in this bowl, where oddities play,
Every fleeting moment is turned into a sway.
With laughter and quirks, it's a riot that's true,
In this vivid escape, we all live anew.

Emergence in a Glassy Alcove

Enclosed in this sphere, shenanigans reign,
Frogs croak and dance, embracing the rain.
Tiny lizards leap, a comedic ballet,
While I sit and chuckle, sipping lemonade.

The daisies bicker over who's the best bloom,
Ignoring the orchid, stuck in its gloom.
Crickets snap selfies with a washed-out grin,
In this glassy space, wild adventures begin.

A mouse with a monocle conducts a show,
As vases and shells compete for the glow.
Every nook holds secrets wrapped up as a joke,
In this quirky habitat, laughter's bespoke.

So raise your glass high to the flora, the fun,
In this jar of oddities, we're never done.
Where moments are silly, and joy's the king,
Here's to the chaos that garden ghosts bring!

Breezes in a Bottled World

In a jar of dreams, the winds rumble free,
As leaves whisper secrets, just between us three.
A parakeet squawks about the latest craze,
While the spider weaves tales in a silken haze.

Mice in tuxedos debate on their cheese,
While ants throw a party, if you please!
A rainbow of petals sings songs on repeat,
With the moon as a DJ, it's an eclectic beat.

Feathers and ferns share a gossip or two,
As fireflies collaborate on a dance debut.
In this bottled up bliss, silliness sows,
As the sun gives a wink, and the wild laughter flows.

From rattling seeds to jocular blooms,
Every inch of the glass is bursting with zooms.
So let's toast to the merriment wrapped in green,
In this bottled world, where joy reigns supreme.

Frolic of Flora Under Glass

Under glassy skies, the flowers conspire,
With petals a-flutter, they spark the desire.
Rabbits in bowties host weekly debates,
As the daisies gossip and the pansies await.

An outrageous cactus takes the prize for puns,
With quips that land softer than springtime runs.
And turtles in shades trot with grand finesse,
While beetles shed tears of cheerful excess.

Laughter erupts as leaves shimmy and sway,
With breezes that tickle in a light-hearted way.
Squirrels invite everyone for a grand feast,
As laughter and mirth multiply, never ceased.

So here in this realm, where humor is king,
Amidst the green chaos, let the joy take wing.
Each tiny adventure makes the heart grow lighter,
In the frolic of flora, the fun feels brighter.

Eclipsed by Glass

A tiny world behind a sheet,
Where plants and critters softly meet.
The snail moves slow, the ant will dash,
Who knew glass walls would spark such clash?

In a bubble where all can stare,
The frog gives side-eye, 'is this fair?'
With curious eyes peeking within,
Each moment is framed; a tidy win.

Grounded by Green

A leafy friend grows quite absurd,
Waving 'hello!' without a word.
The soil's rich, with secrets to share,
Yet ants debate, 'Is this really fair?'

A dance of roots, a tug-of-war,
Barely a battle, but oh, the lore!
With laughter echoing through the rim,
Nature's comedy stays on a whim.

Moments Stilled Within the Glass

Captured here like time lapsed right,
The tiny dwellers stir with fright.
Each glance at moss feels like a tease,
As critters dodge while munching leaves.

A cactus poses, arms held high,
While a beetle wonders, 'Why am I?'
A dance of fate, a twist of grace,
In this box, we all find our place.

Tides of Life in a Captured Scene

Water's waves make ripples appear,
The fish wears spectacles, oh dear!
With bubbles drifting to expand,
Each creature caters to the band.

A shrimp gives wink to a swimming snail,
'You think you're fast? Oh, you'll fail!'
But giggles swell like tides at bay,
In this tiny range, fun leads the way.

Crystalline Cosmos of Nurtured Splendor

A glitter dome locks in the jest,
With every leaf, it's nature's fest.
The worm with dreams of long-lost skies,
Crafts tales in dirt dressed in disguise.

Tiny critters spin stories true,
While the light filters like morning dew.
Within this glass, the mischief's grand,
In a world that's small, yet so well planned.

www.ingramcontent.com/pod-product-compliance
Lightning Source LLC
Chambersburg PA
CBHW070324120526
44590CB00017B/2810